INVISIBLE SELLING

THIS IS A STORY ABOUT HOW I LEARNED TO MARKET IN A LOW-TRUST WORLD

Bojan Mihajlovic

2019. 1st edition

Website: www.bojanmihajlovic.com

Email: b.mihajlovic@me.com

Design by Bojan Mihajlovic

Editing by Crystal Angeles Mihajlovic

We rise by lifting others.

I dedicate this book and this story to my brother Goran.

Once upon a time, there was a man who was proficient in the use of bow and arrow. Whenever he pulled the arrow he hit the center of the target. It could have never happened that he missed the center of the target. Giving the fact that he was the best, he decided to find someone who could do the same, who could hit the center of the target flawlessly. He visited various countries, cities but he didn't find anyone who was skillful as he was. But suddenly he went to a small village located in the woods, and he came across the trees, from which the targets were hanging, and all arrows were pinned in the center. He was amazed because he found someone who was not only skillful as he was but who also lived in a small village. He asked the local villagers who were able to do that and they sent him to a house where one person possessing such skills lived. He wanted to know how this person managed not to make a single mistake just like him. The person he thought was very skillful replied that it was very easy and that everyone could do the same. "you just have to pull the arrow and then to draw the target around the arrow, so that it looks like that arrow is positioned in the center of the target.", said the person.

TABLE OF CONTENTS

Preface

During my long-term career in different areas of business, I noticed that people are familiar only with the basic terms of marketing and knowledge about this important field is not being improved. I have worked in many large companies, received education locally and abroad, but I started truly progressing in my marketing career after my mentoring with Mr Martin Tamm. Martin gave me many guidelines and advice that opened my eyes to education that I was missing. That is when I worked for InterContinental Hotels Group and was trusted with being the project manager. Both then and today, when I am advising new investors, companies, entrepreneurs and CEOs on how to improve their business, I notice that they all have same doubts about marketing. This book includes all the questions and answers that are based on long-term research and my own experiences. I wrote it to help investors, entrepreneurs, CEOs, marketing managers, brand managers, students and those who wish to improve their personal development. The book is a concise manual, without any complicated definitions, that goes to the core of modern age marketing.

MY BEGINNINGS

During the time when I was working at InterContinental Hotel in Belgrade, I managed to attract the attention of an influential person named Martin Tamm. He was the main consultant under the InterContinental Hotels Group and was responsible for opening a new hotel in Belgrade, Serbia. Martin Tamm's name is well known worldwide in the hotel management world and he had also been the marketing manager for the city of Cologne.

I had the honor to have Mr Martin Tamm notice my desire to improve and tenacity to accept challenges. I quickly found out that Mr Martin Tamm is a remarkable professional as well as a marketing expert, and that he is only interested in discipline, dedication, quality and the final results. This is when he decided to take me under his wings and help me improve.

He did not ask me if I was ready, he just flooded me right away with emails, phone calls, messages and meetings like no one else had done before. Back then I was involved in business organization, planning, implementation of marketing activities, sales development, revenue management, budgeting, HR management issues and controlled task execution. At the internal management meeting that had been held on a daily basis, I was expected to envision new strategies necessary to further business development, while at the same time I had to make those strategies precise and effective with return on investment. I knew that staying at the top was immeasurably harder than reaching it. The business system I had been working on was huge and I always had to share my creative ideas with senior managers.

I was aware that my position had reached its peak and I could not maintain the position if business was not profitable. I had often considered and referred to the marketing knowledge I had attained and the best way to make profit. It was tough finding all the answers, figuring out the right ones and justifying the expectations of the position given to me.

During that time, there were many leaders in the company I was working with. These Leaders would quickly seize the highest position and then disappear from it just as quickly, as if they never existed. However, there were some that would make the most of their opportunity, not knowing that there wouldn't be a second chance.

There isn't a second chance to make a first impression in the world of marketing. Many managers that I have come across misuse their first opportunity and eventually lose their reputation and credibility. While people in the business world would perceive small mistakes as insignificant, managers in marketing agree that each mistake is a poor investment. I had to figure out how to avoid mistakes to keep my position at the top of management.

On another typical Monday morning as I was headed to work, I had no clue that everything was about to change in my life. Office Manager informed me that I would get a new and larger office. I was very surprised how fast everything was unfolding. When I entered my new office, I sat in a large comfortable chair and began thinking harder than ever. There was a letter waiting for me on my desk. Mr. Martin Tamm had left me a message on a binder that said to read everything thoroughly, complete all directions and fulfill every task as instructed.

The first page had the title: **INVISIBLE SELLING**

After further reading I realized that this binder contained everything I needed to know about marketing. I found key guidelines that applied to every type of business, not only hotel marketing. It was also mentioned that, based on my potential, he expected to see my efforts make results. He requested that I complete my knowledge by updating myself through educational trainings and in depth research, which is a recipe for a long-term perspective.

Instead of talking every day, Mr. Martin Tamm suggested that I start reading and analyzing future projects that I would be involved in. I also needed to find and read all books on marketing without any extra help or guidance. He brought my attention to the importance of the current market and why I should analyze and compare it to the past several decades. The modern age makes people analyze things in short-term. People lose interest as soon as something new comes to the market and they quickly forget what was there before.

'Be the change you want to see in the world.' (Mahatma Gandhi)

I read this quote more than a dozen times while sitting alone in my office.

I am used to the idea that when you acquire a significant position, you are obliged to give something in return. I had been thinking long and hard that if someone shares some knowledge with me, what is it that I am obliged to give in return.

In moments like this, I never dreamed that I would become a renowned marketing expert and one of the most successful managers in the future.

MARKETING

On the day that I opened the binder, I started analyzing the first task that Mr. Tamm wrote. It was referencing the core of marketing and how to influence.

I immediately scheduled that day to talk with the sales and marketing team that I managed. Our conversation was about improving sales of hotel accommodation occupancy. Time was running out and my associates were loading me up with a bunch of questions that had to deal with positioning our brand and services on the market, distribution channels, reducing our expenses, competition, demands and the behavior of future guests so as to determine the target group.

I felt startled and realized that I needed to find special terminologies and to decipher all the words usually connected with the term marketing in order to explain it clearly to the team.

Mr. Martin Tamm had told me that once I started to understand all the marketing expressions in the books, I would be able to explain it without hesitating.

After thinking about everything Martin told me, I realized that I needed a lot more than the basic terms and definitions.

One of the traditional definitions of marketing tells us that marketing is a number of activities used towards guiding the flux of products and services from the producer to the consumer.

In marketing, it is very important to present things in a simple way and achieve the wanted speed of realization (e.g. the readiness of the customer to buy a product.)

Marketing is like doing a puzzle. By looking for the parts to fit in you are putting together the full picture. If someone were doing a puzzle, the person who first found the right parts and completed the picture would be the winner. If you wished to become a marketing connoisseur, you would need to be able to do the puzzle quickly - that is to say, you would need to be able to briefly present your idea.

A product or a service should be your starting point. Firstly, you need to stir up the public by creating a problem, after which you offer your product or a service as a solution to that problem. When customers find themselves in a situation where your product or a service is necessary for the solution of their problem, they will accept your offer immediately. If you wish to offer a completely new product or a service, first mention some outdated solutions to the customer in order to point out the novelties of your new product. If there are too many competitors on the market for your product or service, the key is to stay focused, figure out an original angle and make sure not to speak negative about your competitors.

Up until 1968, Marlboro cigarettes had been considered to be 'girly cigarettes'. Phillip Morris, the CEO, demanded something new that would bring more efficient results in cigarette sales. By using the marketing campaign called The Last Marlboro Man, they changed their target group and they started reaching out to men, too. After this campaign, they became the number one brand in filter cigarette sales. Until then, they had been number 19 on that list.

The following question that Phillip Morris asked, after the successful campaign, is the question that many forget to ask the moment they reach the top.

What is it that we need to do in the future so that we stay on top forever?

I will give an answer to that question based on my own experience.

Let's start with the marketing plan and the budget.
When you define the term 'marketing', you are considering what needs to be improved right from the very beginning, and then you figure out what is the most efficient way of spending the defined budget.

I noticed that companies, especially the ones that sell more products, spend a lot of money. This poses a question whether each product should have its own budget, as opposed to one big budget for everything. There should be a defined budget for each product so that the marketing expenses can be figured out. The products with lower sales rates get to spend less money on marketing. The products with the highest sales rates get a big budget even though they don't need that much money for it.

It is necessary to make realistic plans and be brutally honest. Don't mix wishes and needs, but rather determine the value of your product or service in comparison with the products and services of your competitors, and how that affects the consumers and the market itself. Furthermore, estimate your possibilities and do the math. Analyze whether the product or service can become more expensive, whether you have the ability to be the leader and the amount of time you had been present on the market.

You need to figure out what would be the most profitable outcome for you. Deal with the competitors in detail because the weaker they are, the stronger you are.

Lastly, target your advertisements to the people it will affect the most, because you'll realize that you spend the most money on advertisements. Advertisement will not help you if you only want to convince the customers, change their opinion, or if you only want to draw their attention to the way you differ from others. Additionally, you need to learn when to STOP if your budget keeps decreasing. Do not be impatient, but rather concentrate on what you will get in return when you launch the product or the service.

Based on all these details I analyzed, I realized that the key point is to plan everything out perfectly in order to get results. I attract customers, I need to cherish and keep them. That way I am showing them that I respect their opinion and that I am always there when they need me to provide the right product or service. The time spent on searching for new clients is much longer than the time spent on keeping the existing clients. Long time ago, selling was basically loading up your products in a bag, putting them out in a public place and waiting for the people to come and buy them. Today the situation is much more different. In distribution, the most important thing is selling directly to people and avoiding selling a product or a service through a third party.

When a hotel sales manager sells rooms via a booking.com portal, which operates as an online travel agency, he has to pay the commission fee. That way sales manager also gives up a small share of his profit. On the other hand, if sales manager sells the rooms directly to the clients, he has complete control of the selling process, represents his product or services, and also gets a bigger profit.

Things are never as simple as they may seem. You have a great idea and you immediately think that it is a winning one. In the car industry you will notice that they are making a better model of a car than the previous model, and in the Hotel industry you will notice they are building more modern and up to date hotels than their competitors. However, you will not consider the failures of these companies. This is an important area that must be analyzed and considered.

Always estimate both successes and failures of your competitors - it can be the right guideline for your marketing strategy.

MARKETING MIX

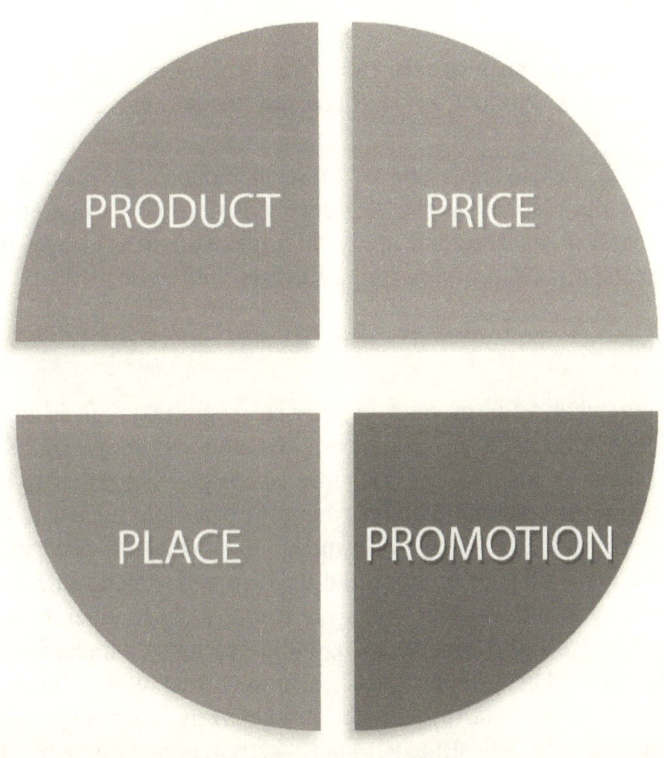

The next day, I read the following topic in the marketing mix binder that Martin left on my desk. I realized that marketing is a group of predefined steps and processes that we need to do in order to achieve connection with the market, it's the way to exchange offers valuable to guests, consumers, clients, partners and society itself.

This activity consists of four interconnected elements, that is called marketing mix. Product, Price, Place and Promotion

When it comes to each one of these elements, you need to make decisions that depend on the elements' position in the market. If you often reassess, analyze and apply this mix, you secure loyal guests, consumers, clients, partners and customers.

Product

Deciding what your product or service is going to be is only the beginning. You need to further plan, develop and strategize. No one expects you to make all the decisions overnight, but rather to have a clear vision in your mind about what you want and what you do not want. Additionally, you will need to think of the physical characteristics of your product like the size and structure or the type of service you will provide and what it will include. Each product is a story for itself and consists of its looks, various characteristics and functionality. The product package is specified with a number of sales activities, starting with transporting, storage, product presentation and adjustments. These activities will depend on the number of customers to expect, which will help you know how much capacity you will require, to make the process easier. Many products have a seasonal consumption and many have high standards to keep in stock. There are also world known brands that have policies for adjusting the price of their products, whereby they reduce the quality or price so that the product is more accessible to all customers.

Price

Define a price and it changes in regards to the product or service. Everything has to have its dynamics and logic. Think and make decisions about price strategies according to seasons, purchasing in advance, in installments, at clearance sales, in bundles, target clients or VIP customers. Never neglect current customers because you can always up sale or stimulate them with a reasonable price to want to purchase more.

Place

Place is the location where you will sell your product and services. Whether it is going to be an offline or online store it will depend on the distribution strategy. Your business is as powerful as your distribution network. Place should have a wide network through a number of channels that functions independently.

Promotion

Promotion should include everything, starting from the communication with the customers, future customers, or partners. It should include the social media activities as well. Marketing mix is important because it affects the society we live in and the success or failure of our company. It needs to be adapted to the users, services and the buyers of our products to create a certain advantage that all segments are well combined, well-coordinated and incorporated into the company.

BRAND

Mr. Martin Tamm was surprised by the progress I was making with my ideas on marketing. Above all, I really wanted to impress him. I had been reading all the books on branding I could find in the market, I visited seminars, watched video courses and participated in webinars in order to find out what my next progress.

Everywhere I went I would come across one subject that started to impose itself as the next one, branding.

The point of branding is to make your product stand out in regards to other products similar to yours, and also to create a unique perception of your product by keeping in mind of your customers wants and needs in order for them to choose your product. Branding is the creation of a unique and positive impression, perception and emotion in the mind of the client or customer, thus making an influence on them.

A long time ago, companies used to have their logo or just the name of the product displayed, but today every brand manager is trying to develop brand on new way. In essence, this complicated job, as the marketing consultants call it, only creates more and more brands, and barely anyone thinks about whether they bring positive or negative results. In order to succeed in the sea of well-known names in business, the most important thing is to stand out with a good name for your brand.

Every brand appears in the mind of the consumer and represents the name of its product. If you have a catchy easy to remember name, you have a big advantage. The wrong brand name can destroy you. There are numerous examples of bad brand names that no one remembers anymore.

There are plenty huge companies that have had bad brand names that no one will remember even if they were successful in business. Also, there are companies that, with the goal of being more innovative, have turned their brand into nonsense by using numbers, initials or something that does not have anything to do with the product they are selling.

Choosing a good name is not an easy task. You need to be careful on choosing a name. Avoid using a cliché, weird or your last name. The name of your brand should be directly connected to your product or service. It is dangerous to give an unusual or even weird name to your brand – it is best for it to be pleasant or well thought out.

Making a brand makes a big difference for your product or service compared to those used by your competitors. If you equal your brand to the existing one, and you are in no way different than them, your price then needs to be lower.

Studies have shown that after some time, leading brands on the market start to become similar to one another. This happens because marketing experts promote and represent their products and services and do not build their brand. Then, by advertising they inform but not emphasize how different they are from others. They are not branding, they are just concerned with prices. Many marketing managers promote absurd slogans and think that it is enough for their products and services to look new and better to get a better position in the market.

This approach is wrong. The idea is to be unique and different, by using completely different activities than your competitors in search of performances that are not directly correlated with the product or service. Branding is forming a brand based on the differences from the viewpoint of the consumers.

The first part is to make a brand, but the real question is how to stop destroy the own brand. Usually, those who work without any plans and goals make these kinds of mistakes. They destroy their main brand by making sub-brands.

Hyundai is trying to sell cars of smaller dimensions in Europe, while Porsche is trying to sell SUV's. They think that this way they will strengthen their position on the market and make more profit. But the more cheap cars they sell, the more they destroy their brand's prestige.

All this does not mean that we should not represent our brands in different ways. It is crucial not to step away from the main point of our brand, because the brand is a promise, which evokes certain expectations that the products and services needs to fulfill.

If the tennis racket made by Wilson is used by Roger Federer and is intended for tennis players, what purpose would a Wilson soccer ball have? There would be a purpose if the manufacturer made a soccer ball that Cristiano Ronaldo would use, but then it would no longer be a Wilson soccer ball but rather a Cristiano Ronaldo soccer ball.

Something that happens very often in practice is when a famous company or investor with a big appetite wants to own a brand through a franchise. This would satisfy the investors' ego and the demands of certain markets. The real truth is that realistic possibilities do not often allow an adequate profit for it.

Prestige hotel chains are parts of funds owned by small groups of investors. Their representatives in different and smaller locations sell the franchises or management contracts and they make profit for that. In their cases it is less important whether the hotels do profitable business or not – it is only important to respect a certain standard. Franchises usually buy companies that have money or the possibility to stand out in those locations using a well-known hotel brand; they also get a certain standard and quality, while at the same time they can brag about owning a brand. Although they are not aware of this, fund investors affect prestige hotel chains so much that they become less prestige over time. In this case we need to make special effort to keep and protect a brand from those led by greed.

Taking all of this into account, we need to avoid greed and always be aware of the fact that we need to sacrifice some things in order to keep a brand alive. Sacrificing can refer to staying focused on one type of product. Ferrero produces only one type of sweets and Spirit airline only offers low cost flights. Additionally, this can refer to defining only one characteristic of your product or service.

Apple focuses mainly on quality, while Ferrari focuses on prestige.

Your other option is to make a sacrifice for the target market and be the primary choice for buying.

Potbelly is a restaurant chain that primarily serves sandwiches and Bentley products are only intended for the wealthy.

My conclusion is to stay focused on what the brand means to your consumers.

LOGO

Mr. Tamm and I went for lunch at a sushi restaurant for the weekend, we realized that we like the same food and of course we could not help but talk about work. He brought my attention to the fact that I should update my knowledge on logos.

Logos have had their influence ever since people used clay tablets and war symbols. All of them are long forgotten, we can now only remember the names that made a big impact in history. I realized that the point was not in the symbol itself but in its connection to the name. The greatness of the brand is in its name and not its symbol.

All around us we can see both well and badly designed logos. Again, large sums of money are spent on them, which poses the question whether that money is being poured down the drain. It takes many years for the logo to become known in the world, and without a name it does not have a chance at all.

If we focus too much on designing a logo that it becomes unrecognizable and illegible, the symbol cannot have a desired effect. The most important things about logos are the shape, color and abbreviation.

For starters, you should pick the right color for your logo, and it would be best if it were only one color, because people after some time start to connect that color with your brand. The shape becomes the identity of your brand over time and choosing the right color should make your brand stand out from the brands of your competitors.

The logo can be an abbreviation that says something about your brand, but those initials should also have a meaning behind them. If the customers remember the full name of your brand, that should also be the logo. The market demands the nicknames or the initials. Think more about the psychology of logo designing.
Since we are all human beings, our brain recognizes shapes. The shape of our logo is of immense importance. Each letter should be

individually designed and connected to one another, and also the shape of the logo should be connected to the meaning and the sound.

Many designers are only concerned with aesthetics. Designing a logo is so much more, it represents certain psychology that the design carries with it. Designers need to communicate with their future customers through their creations and visual identities that are being created. While designing a logo, it is not good to only focus on our current feelings, but rather to try and take a look at the future.

In the late '90s in New York City, I perfected my knowledge on logo designing. I was lucky because based on my knowledge from back then, I can design any logo today. If you're not knowledgeable about this topic as you should be, I would recommend that you leave this task to a professional designer.

RESEARCH

By looking over the topics in the folder I came across marketing planning, budgeting, and a section on research. I noticed that a large sum of money is being spent on research. Today, apart from the usual surveys, questionnaires and target plans there are also other experimental techniques to find out people's thoughts. Market research spends a lot of time, energy and money in order to hear people's voice. The real question is, have those techniques ever helped a struggling company? When you hand out such a review to a manager, he does not even glance at it. If he reads by any chance a small portion of the text, what attracts his attention is only something that supports his moves.

Advertising agencies also do some researching in order to impress their clients. I was thinking about whether I should cancel the budget for that kind of research. The question is not simple and I must say that the answer is no different. The only thing I can say for sure is that we need to take out practical information from people. However, when you try to get an accurate piece of information, you encounter a problem where people are not honest enough. If you ask a customer why they bought your product, you will get more than one answer that is not honest and useful. It is completely clear that people often say one thing and act differently. People are not even aware of what is it that motivates them to buy a product, some maybe even know the answer, but that does not mean that they want to or know how to explain it. We also know that the customer will recognize a brand long after we have stopped advertising it, but making a customer remember can make things seem quite different.

Using the example of public opinion research on choosing a political party to vote for, a large sum of money is being spent on that research, and then the research agency calls a few people for sampling. The agency does not do all the required procedures and the money is wasted. I did a research on my own. My examinees were people I knew of different age groups. The question was which travel agency they would use to organize their trip that year. The results showed that a travel agency that had not even existed for some time was third on the list. Based on this I started to think whether these people even stopped to think before they made decisions. Of course, this is not true, but most people working in marketing do not notice that people buy what they think they need, or the things other people accept as necessary. We watch people every day and we notice that they are not always sure about what they want. Also, people do not want to think too much about anything unless it is about health, money or their sex life. Marketing managers need a quick overview of what the customers think. The managers need to investigate all the pros and cons of the competition the same way the customers see them. One of the good ways for market research is asking the examinees to rank the pros of buying a product on a scale from one to ten. This method can be called diversity research.

As an example we can take women's sanitary pads. There are certain qualities that are characteristic for each brand of pads. Always bases its brand on maximum absorption, Naturella highlights the cotton fabric of the pads and Libresse always offers a nice packaging for storing the pads. In case of successful brands, each one has to have an advantage. The goal is to find out which advantage you will use to attract customers. Market research exists in order to lead the way to

the customer's mind. The market is not being researched in order to find out what the customers want or to deal with their psyche, but rather to measure their perception of the advantages that the brand has in comparison with the competitors' brands. It is hard to predict the future and find out the way to make people buy a product or use a service if they had not seen it before or if someone had not bought it before them. We cannot plan out our day-to-day steps, but we can observe recent trends and that way not fall behind the newest things.
If the current trend in US is a healthy lifestyle, that trend should be the one we base our product on. Following the trend may also be uncertain, but you should always remember that unexpected things can always happen, and that it is impossible to explore the unexpected. All this made me reduce the budget for the research. The research can get good results if it is simple.

STRATEGY

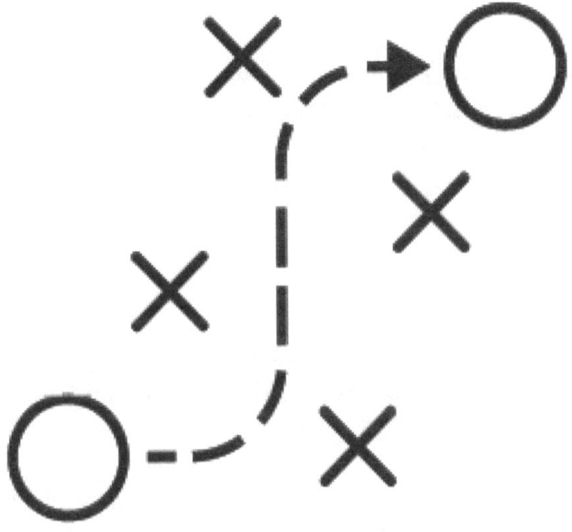

The most important detail for each leader is to strategically position themselves on the market. The term strategy includes the plan that is formed and defined with the purpose of goal realization.

After having read various articles and literature on strategic marketing, I could clearly state that 90% of new products and services fail on the market. Based on my experience and statistics, I had to ask myself which products and services I should approve and which ones I should not.

I remember the time when the Hotel in Belgrade had lost its franchise and was forced to form a new name and a new brand. The people working in marketing had not stopped in their never-ending attempt to alter and build up the existing brand. It seemed like all the alterations were being done in moments of idleness.

Certain experts in other fields confuse the minds of their future customers with the desire to improve their offer on the market. In order not to make another disastrous product or service, I realized that our brand had to be either first or second in the market, or another innovation would have to appear.

The basic task of marketing is to provide the number one position for the brand. The law of leadership says that it is better to be first than to be better. We need to check the pulse of our target category and appear first on the market. That way the name of the brand becomes the name of the whole category.

The leading brands that appeared first on the market were Bambi as the first manufacturer of biscuits and sweet pastries in ex-Yugoslavia, who soon started producing Plazma-Lane, and Red Bull that appeared on the market in 1987 as a completely new product, that way forming a whole new category of products.

The new age has brought new trends that I needed to fit in fast. My co-workers could not understand why it was so important to follow the novelties on the market as well as the new principles and demands of the consumers of our products. During that time, since I was familiar with programming, I decisively directed my business towards online marketing. I segmented the sales to selling services using credit cards. I launched this project in collaboration with Banca Intesa. It was tough animating the customers to get their trust so they start using websites to pay for services. Eventually, the project was a success. Up until then, no one in Serbia had ever known how to use credit cards for paying online. We had to make our customers feel confident and secure about using credit cards on our website.

Revenue management has an important role because it refers to the maximization of the profit and is closely related to marketing. For a long time I was the only one promoting services using online travel agencies. Afterwards, I was the first one to use channel manager and rate shopping software. I concluded that if I had a good photo of the bedroom, bathroom, the entire object and if I carefully chose my words for describing the service with good coordination of the prices, I would have the possibility to position myself highly on the market. I noticed that the print media trend is in decline and I could predict that the importance of electronic media would start to increase. More and more people started to book rooms online rather than over the phone or at the hotel reception. No one could fully understand what I was doing back then, but today everyone can see the future estimation on their own.

Making good estimations and using good strategy have contributed to the fact that we have full capacity occupancy most of the time. In accordance with this step, the hotel has become significantly dominant compared to the competition.

Efficiently directing the customers towards booking rooms using websites as well as income increase have brought me the collaboration with booking.com. I have become a part of their development team and have contributed to the growth of the extranet system for the Balkans region.

Extraordinary leaders always have new ideas that disarm their competition. Every couple of years they switch their old products with brand-new ones, that way keeping their market stable for a long time.

For example, Nivea has something new to offer every year - anti-aging cream, night cream or moisturizing cream.

However, what happens if the competition already has a leading product or a service?

In that case, that company has to offer either product number two or an alternative that must not offer the same as the primary product.

You can always be the first even if you are currently the second by developing an efficient alternative strategy and finding a different target group inside of the primary product.

In order to resist the success of Mercedes-Benz, BMW directed their sales towards the younger target group.

According to the product strategy, you can become successful either if you are the first or the second, while the third position is uncertain and the fourth unsuccessful.

There is a law of duality in marketing. There are always two products in a race - Adidas and Nike, ATT and Verizon, Apple and Samsung.

There is always a fight on the market between a long-lasting brand and a new one.

The fight is the most interesting when both brands are the leaders and all the comments are directed towards which one is better. That is when you should interest the customers with a new idea.

In marketing we call that market segmentation.

Each company perceives the brand from the economic point of view.

For that reason they are ready to expand their selection of products. If they get too much into expanding the selection, the brand can lose its value.

My advice is that you should avoid similar products or services and never-ending selection expanding. Leading products are the ones that are either the first or the second in a certain category or the ones that start a new sub-category.

PRICE

The moment people start trading, the price becomes the main subject. Many people say that something is worth only the amount of money that people are ready to pay for it. As simple as it may sound, today it is much more complicated than that. Firstly, you need to stay in the game long enough in regard to the competition, as well as be conscious of the fact that people are ready to pay even more if they get the impression that something is valuable. The amount that a client is ready to pay represents the price of a product or a service. If we attempt to make the client pay more for a certain product or a service, he may wonder whether he is paying too much. In case such a thing happens, the competition may take the lead and push you out of the way from the market.

One of the ideas I implemented was the weekend brunch. I defined a price of $9 per person. Children up to ten years old could use the service plus entertainment free of charge. My co-workers stated that the price was formed below its value. I understood what they meant by it, however, I had a clear vision in my mind about my goal. I trained the waiters to sell drinks at a much higher price that was not included in the service. That way I made a balance and got extra income. I actively included the guests into talking about a meal at a reasonable price at a well-known location accessible only to people with high income.

The psychological 'catch' I knew that my co-workers did not know that each person that visits us for the first time is our biggest expense. When the guest returns for the second time, everything is being directed towards the goal. That guest brings over his friends because he was satisfied with the service, thus spreading the recommendation. The guest that comes for the second time eats much less because his main intention is to show off to his friends his creative choices, and after a while starts to bring over an entire army of guests. This strategy fills the capacity in the long run. After that we start to slowly raise the prices, while letting the people keep spending time with their families and enjoying quality food. Everything else is the PWOM effect (positive word-of-mouth). Additionally, people are always ready to pay a little more money if they are aware that a product or a service is more valuable. As long as you keep your existence on the market and your clients feel that what they buy is more valuable, your place is secure and guaranteed. The client expects to pay more if he is aware of the quality of the product.

I can say from my own experience that if I buy a Colmar jacket at a higher price, I am positive that the fabric will be of high quality. If you buy an Audi car and you pay a lot of money for it, you want the people around you to know that you are successful. When a new competitor appears on the market of these prestigious brands, they attack you with the pricing. They usually use a lower price to attract new customers, but you cannot let such a competitor come to the market, and the only thing you can do is find a new way to defend your prices. We come to the conclusion that high prices and huge profit attracts competition. They notice your success and try to take some of the profit away from you. The global discount supermarket chain Aldi, uses the well-known pricing strategy when it appears on the market by acquiring a big quantity of a certain product and selling it at a considerably lower price, sometimes even consciously below its value. That way Aldi attracts a crowd of customers that come to buy that product but also buy all the other products. Aldi raises the prices for all the other products in the way the customer does not even notice. The companies that think intelligently do not exhaust the market, they rather keep the prices low in order to become dominant and destroy the competition.

Google learned this lesson the hard way when they gave away free online services in order to push the competition away. They got a lot of lawsuits because of this move and they had to spend a lot of money on all the trials and negotiations. It is always better to direct your energy to making new products and implementing marketing strategies. It is one thing when you conquer the market with your high prices, but it is not easy to win if you use the low pricing strategy. It is absurd if you lower the price too much and if the competitors can lower it as much as you can. In the future development of the company, I had noticed that, after my instructions, no one even mentioned lowering the prices, they rather used diversity and adding value in order to justify the price.

GROWTH OR GREED

I reached the point where I started to analyze the results of my colleagues which had managed the business in the previous period. I started to think whether it was smart to keep being enthusiastic about the potential on the market or if we should just insist on growing our business.

The continual desire for growth makes the company managers turn to greed since they constantly make the company grow in order to secure their reputation and increase their own profit. The largest number of mistakes in marketing is the result of this desire.

Facebook social network, the year of appearing on the market was the year of great potential. It was expected that the number of users will reach one billion. The appearance on the market was impatiently waited for with great enthusiasm. However, the market had brought a bad initial effect on Facebook. The estimated worth of $100 billion had proved to be overrated, and lawsuits against Facebook, Mark Zuckerberg and the banks that had been cooperating with them during the initial stock offer followed. Also, the media started to attack Zuckerberg who, once a likeable boy next door, had become a greedy owner overnight. Instead of the development of the pricing of the stocks, all the people who had wanted a quick profit were met with shock and short term growth. For weeks Facebook's stocks had been dropping, and at one point it lost more than half of its total worth. That way in only a few months Facebook had lost tens of thousands of dollars, while Mark Zuckerberg had lost similar amount of money, and the employees of the company had lost around two million dollars. Many experts went so far as to say that Facebook's appearance on the stock market was the beginning of the end of this company. Many managers are considered to be irresponsibly greedy because they are usually oriented towards the value of the stocks rather than the market and their main strategy is to make more profit.

You should never focus on the profit but on building your brand because the brand is the one that needs a long term perspective. It is important to think thoroughly about the basic rules of making a brand and all the ways to stop yourself from crossing any lines. The most important thing is not to run away from your main business. If you ever step outside from the main business and expand the offer on the market with new products and services, you need to be very careful since this way of thinking may lead you to the wrong direction.

Long time ago, only the big agencies would do the advertising. Today everyone can try to do that. If you have a good product or a service but you do not have the person who can advertise the product or run the business, you are in big trouble. If we take Hermès or Armani fashion industry as an example, we can see that only Hermès has good advertising which is directed towards luxury. Armani has tried to mix luxury and mass market brand in order to appeal to more customers. This is how many Armani collections have appeared on the market. They have started to create collections of considerably lower quality than expected. On the other hand, Hermès has still continued to make their first class collections. They never wanted to appear on the mass market, but rather to continue being a luxurious brand. Staying focused in marketing is an outstanding recipe for success. It is always more efficient to be realistic than to be led by desire for growth. Good leaders stay true to themselves, do not give way to illusions, they set up realistic goals and motivate people. Irrelevant things are not needed in marketing.

BMW has always been at the top of the list of first class cars. Porsche has always been selling sports cars. If you always try to appeal to everyone, you will lose focus. Setting up realistic plans makes a difference between what can be done and what we wish for.

Do not be guided by the ambitions of the stock market. Always be brutally honest and fair. Successful leaders are not obsessed with growth but with their success in the market.

ADVERTISING

We managed to agree on the budget for the research. I saw from the financial reports that large sums of money were being spent on advertising and I wondered whether I should support the decision on spending a lot or suggest a new plan. My co-workers presented their appealing suggestions and presentations using a lot of charts and images and it all required a lot of money to be prepared, let alone carried out. My task was to estimate the effects of the advertising suggestions. Advertising is what we do when we cannot talk to the client in person – we present them a printed, TV or online advertisement and we tell our story. We start each story with an introduction in which we state why we are different from the competition, why they should buy the product or service from us and then say our slogan. The message in advertisement should announce the difference between our product, the competitors' products and all its benefits. It is crucial to direct the right emotions towards the target customers that watch or analyze the advertisement. The emotion of the message we send can lead to either contentment or pain. The energy we transmit can be high positive or low positive as well as high negative or low negative. High positive energy is happiness and contentment, while low positive is bliss. High negative energy is rage, sadness or misfortune while low negative is disappointment.

For example, we want to offer winter tires for cars to a wide mass of people. In the first advertisement we make a scenario of a happy family in a car on the snow and a content and proud father with a big smile on his face while he is driving the car on an icy hill. The expression on his face leaves a great effect on the person watching the advertisement and safely brings the family to the destination while the children enjoy the car. In the end there is a message with the accent on happiness and contentment: Buy your tires on time.

In the second advertisement we make the same scenario with the family in the car going on a trip and they face the obstacle, snow on the uphill, which quickly leads to slipping and falling into the abyss. This way we show the people that accidents can happen and we make an influence on them so they start to think about the possible circumstances such as sadness and misfortune. In the end of the advertisement we also send the same message: Buy your tires on time. In Serbia and the surrounding countries the second option is much more efficient. People like advertisements because they are fun and informative. In advertisements we can use humor and sex and whatever comes to our mind, but we have to state the reason why someone should buy the product.

One of the examples of an advertisement that really makes an impact on the viewers is the commercial for Lav beer, in which the actor Nenad Jezdic plays the best man at a wedding. His friends ask him what presents did the newlyweds receive as he toasts with the beer and alludes that he is a Lav (lion) since he had given a car as a present. The dramatization of each scene is outstanding. Great as your advertisement may be, if you release it on TV in the middle of an interesting movie or a match, no one would be happy that you did it. This is why you need to bring a bit of honesty in your advertisements.

The customers will give you positive feedback if you are being honest with them. If the product that you advertise is of too large dimensions and that product should be of domestic use, be honest and admit it, and then highlight its reliability. Honesty may be one of the main preconditions that your advertisement stays being accepted by the public. This is just one part of it. What you need to do is make your advertisement seem like it is something completely new on the market. The customers are always looking for something new. The viewers of the commercials will not watch them with full attention if they are watching something that is too complicated. This is why your commercials should always be simple and the words in the message should rhyme if possible, because people will remember them better, and the fastest way to the brain is sound. Additionally, the commercials should be clear and state a clear idea. And lastly, you need to be patient – the moment your repetitive message starts to be annoying, the customer will start to remember it. If your commercial seems perfect to you, talk to a friend and listen to another point of view.

MEDIA

Many years ago there was only printed media, which was followed by radio, TV and internet. It has become difficult to choose the media to use. Also, you can now see an advertisement everywhere, on the sides of buses, in elevators, on clothes, billboards, planes, doctor's offices and even in the toilets. Making a choice means understanding the advantages and weaknesses of each medium. Firstly, we rely on the number of people that will see our advertisement, and in this sense the internet has a slight advantage because it allows a detailed targeting through popular social networks such as Facebook, Instagram, Twitter, LinkedIn and Pinterest. The dominant Google offers an entire collection of marketing tools, from using analytics for its own website to using algorithms where you have the option to be found on Google search if you respect the code. YouTube gives you the option to talk to the possible customers through visualization and video content. You can also choose the option do get through to the developed and popular portals. There are also various smartphone apps that many people use today as well. Radio has an important role too. A TV commercial may stop someone from what they were doing in order to give them the intended message, and it can have an extraordinary effect if it is efficient enough.

Smartphones that use Android or iOS operating systems allow you to get through to the target customers using text message or video messages through an incentive program or a giveaway.

The post office can also cover a great number of people, but its expenses are bigger if you have a large base of contacts. To the question which one is more powerful, the eye or the ear, the answer is always the same. The eye is more powerful. Probably everyone is led by the quote that a picture is worth a thousand words. TV, movies and the internet sell pictures worth millions of dollars.

Marketing is not only visual but also verbal. It is the program of both ideas and images. You should also be aware that the ear is faster than the eye and that we can hear faster than we see. We remember better the things we heard rather than the things we saw. The image itself, as a representation of the visual, loses its value if our mind does not connect it to an idea. It is much more efficient to hear a message than to just read it. What you say makes you follow the thought more clearly, while at the same time you connect that thought to an emotion. Media that uses sounds are the most important ones, while the written word takes the second place. One of the most important segments is PR and promotion. The target group will react better if they read an appraising text about someone than if they just saw the advertisement.

If the pharmaceutical company sells a inhaler for asthma, they can purchase an advertisement space, but it can also have an article published with the headline The boy who got his asthma cured. The text describes all the benefits of this drug and that way achieves more effective sales, and also makes the customers' conscience filled with a positive experience. There are big differences among the stated media. You can use all the available media, which is called unified marketing. You need to formulate the message, find out the advantages of all of them and use them wisely. The advertisement may secure recognition, PR gives information and credibility, the internet gives all the extra details, the appearance on the fair increases people's interest, the post office appeals to all the important customers and promotion is directed towards the usage of the product or service. If the marketing is integrated, you need to avoid over-promoting because you invite people to bargain if you organize sales with discount prices. We can conclude that in the past the medium that had sound was the dominant one, and that was enough. Today internet has a secure first place in media domination, which represents a unified example of media.

CRM

This is one of the most important business strategies that I have learned at work. Many of my co-workers had some difficulties trying to understand the importance of this system. However, once established, it strengthens loyalty, reduces expenses, increases profitability and satisfaction of the customers, clients, guests and users.

A frequently asked question is whether the integration of this system is related to sales and building the base of contacts or is it used exclusively for marketing purposes. This business strategy is not directed towards only one sector, but it can be used for any sector. Overall, anyone who has clients, customers, guests should most definitely have this system. There are various software available, among which the most prominent ones are Sales Force CRM and Windows Dynamics, even though you can make everything you need using an Excel sheet and neatly keep records of everything. Every day that you come to work you feel insecure because you think that you do not have enough information about people that have already bought something from you - your clients. The data is kept in some folders, drawers, notebooks, and the contact phone numbers of the clients are kept in the phones of all employees, you have some numbers on your desktop about how much money people have spent on a product or service. Some data is in the finance sector, some in the sales department, and the rest is in the marketing sector.

- What happens when some of the employees go on vacation or ask for a day off?
- Where will we find all the important data?
- How do we prepare for the meeting with a new or an existing customer?

- What if the CEO or the owner needs all the important information?

It is crucial to know how to communicate both within the company and with the potential customers. The more information you know about the buyer and the more attention you give them, the bigger are the chances for them to become your loyal customer. This is one of the tasks of CRM. You do not need to wait for a programmer to make a software for you, you can just make everything by yourself easily. Simply put, CRM allows you to make a unique base of contacts in one place that contain all the most important and the most minute details about each and every customer.

What does this base of contacts contain?

- First name, last name, phone number, email, address, client's or company's location
- An overview of the offers and achieved cooperation
- Signed contracts and realized projects
- What they bought
- What they were offered but did not buy
- Extra and special demands
- Impressions of the employees about the customer
- Possibilities about further cooperation

This system allows for the organization of the data and it is available to use at any time. When you hire a new employee, thanks to this base, they are also informed immediately about everything. In every business, we use a lot of data and it is important not to forget or lose it, but it is just as important to use it correctly.

SELF MARKETING

Mastering all the techniques for using social networks in order for your business to get the sign of approval, also known as LIKE, refers to the gist of your job. When you present a good idea, you promote your business, but you do not promote yourself.

If you are not able to sell yourself, then you are not able to sell anything else either. Personal marketing can help you sell yourself more easily and more quickly.

The term of personal marketing or self-marketing is not clearly defined nor defined enough in US. Personal marketing helps the individual improve their image and reputation in order for their career to move forward.

Personal marketing is often referred to as personal branding because the actions are similar as in making a brand. You need to perfect communication skills in which you represent yourself, your value, skills, education, experience and ideas to a potential boss, owner or client. Successful personal marketing is the one that makes you stand out and be more competitive.

There are many strategies in personal marketing.

Social networks allow you to make your own profile where you would state examples of your work, your experience and where you would connect to employers. Blogs and vlogs give you the opportunity to show what you know and make comments about trends on the market. At professional gatherings you can also connect to other employers and leave the image of yourself as part of your personal brand. Even by doing volunteer work you improve your personal brand, you build a positive image of yourself and your values.

Here is some advice about personal branding that can be of help:

- Make personal branding your second job. Work on yourself every day and keep improving your image
- Use social networks Facebook, Instagram, LinkedIn in order to connect with potential bosses or clients
- Find a way to become visible online so that your boss can always find you on the internet
- Use online forums. Join discussions about the market and state your experiences clearly
- Highlight the praises you got about your work
- Choose ten key words about why your work is better than your competitors' on your webpage
- Use key words that lead to your webpage so that clients and HR experts can find you more easily
- Influence your friends to make positive comments on your posts on the internet

There are two types of people that want personal marketing – the first are the ones that are looking for work and the second are the ones that want to stand out.

Letter

When I got the opportunity to get promoted, I had to thank Mr. Martin Tamm that I was so thrilled about all the things that my new position would bring. I had been reading in detail everything left for me in the folder and I was determined to write an email that would contain a summary of everything I had found out and put into practice. The subject of the email was Actions that need to be avoided in marketing.

Dear Mr. Tamm,

Thank you for the given trust and directions to commit to such an important subject as Marketing. As a result of research, consideration and experience I have gained in the past period, I decided to write you an email in which I would state my findings about the actions that need to be avoided in Marketing.

After we gather all the information about marketing that we need in order to define this term, in most cases we pay attention to what we need to do rather than on what we must not do.

I will state all the actions I have concluded that should be avoided in marketing.

Today when people become successful, they stop being objective. They become blinded by their attitude and they stop wearing their customers' shoes – they stop thinking like their customers. We need to avoid the arrogance when we are at the top and make optimal decisions.

The next thing we need to avoid is greed. Management is concentrated on building value, not on the company itself. Greed is spreading like a virus into all sectors of management, and after some time everyone starts making decisions relevant only to their own finances rather than the company's finances.

We should never stop learning and perfecting ourselves. When we stop learning, we stop improving as well.

The next action bad for marketing is unrealistic decisions of the managers. As opposed to them, many successful companies focus on harsh reality and they do not do what they want but what they can.

If a rising company does not do what it knows, the management loses interest and takes up other activities. If you lose focus, you lose the strength of the company.

It is easy noticing mistakes of others but it is hard noticing your own. Pride is the cause of that. The wealthier and the better positioned on the market do not need to underestimate the competition.

Not understanding digital marketing is also one of the bad actions. Every expert in marketing has to follow the trends in digital marketing on a daily basis. The new age demands quick reaction.

You should never forget that working on personal marketing is very important for positioning in any business. You need to build your base of business contacts and know the needs of your clients. Networking is an unbreakable link in improving and building personal image.

I wrote all this and sent it to Mr. Martin Tamm. I got a reply the very same day.

I am certain that your future will be different from your past and I know now that you understand the meaning of the saying

"INVISIBLE SELLING" I believe that you can share your knowledge and experience with the society and help others accomplish their goals when they need support.